Deadliest Diseases of All Time

Tuberculosis

Randall
McPartland

Cavendish
Square
New York

Published in 2016 by Cavendish Square Publishing, LLC
243 5th Avenue, Suite 136, New York, NY 10016

Library of Congress Cataloging-in-Publication Data

McPartland, Randall.
Tuberculosis / Randall McPartland.
pages cm. — (Deadliest diseases of all time)
Includes glossary.
Includes bibliographical references and index.
ISBN 978-1-50260-646-4 (hardcover) ISBN 978-1-50260-647-1 (ebook)
1. Tuberculosis—History—Juvenile literature. 2. Tuberculosis—Treatment—History—Juvenile literature.
I. Title.

RC310.M35 2016
616.99'5—dc23

2014050275

Editorial Director: David McNamara
Editor: Fletcher Doyle
Copy Editor: Cynthia Roby
Art Director: Jeffrey Talbot
Senior Designer: Amy Greenan
Senior Production Manager: Jennifer Ryder-Talbot
Production Editor: Renni Johnson
Photo Researcher: J8 Media

The photographs in this book are used by permission and through the courtesy of: kukhunthod/iStock/Thinkstock, cover
(background; used throughout book); Scott CAamazine/Science Source/Getty Images, cover (inset); Lam Yik Fei/Getty
Images, 4; Rajesh Kumar Singh/AP Images, 7; Anibal Solimano/Getty Images, 8; Cpaulfell/Shutterstock.com, 11; Rufus46/
File:Bayerische Staatsbibliothek Statue des Hippokrates Muenchen-2.jpg/Wikimedia Commons, 12; ManuelVelasco/
iStockphoto.com, 14; New York World-Telegram and the Sun staff photographer: Higgins, Roger/File:Selman Waksman
NYWTS.jpg/Wikimedia Commons, 17; The Print Collector/Getty Images, 18; Popperfoto/Getty Images, 21; Dan Bates/
File:Wyatt and Doc.jpg/Wikimedia Commons, 23; Patrick Branwell Brontë/File:The Brontë Sisters by Patrick Branwell Brontë
restored.jpg/Wikimedia Commons, 27; Leo Rosenthal/Pix Inc./The LIFE Images Collection/Getty Images, 30; NIAID/
File:Mycobacterium tuberculosis MEB.jpg/ Wikimedia Commons, 33; Universal History Archive/Getty Images, 37; RedTC/
Shutterstock.com, 38; JR2009/Shutterstock.com, 39; Alfred Eisenstaedt/The LIFE Picture Collection/Getty Images, 42;
Science Source/Getty Images, 45; BBC/File:George-orwell-BBC.jpg/Wikimedia Commons, 47; Tony Karumba/AFP/Getty
Images, 50; Alexander Raths/Shutterstock.com, 54; Paula Bronstein/Getty Images, 57.

Printed in the United States of America

Contents

Introduction

Tuberculosis, or TB, may be thought of by some as a disease that medical science has sent to the scrapbooks of history. Other infectious diseases, specifically Ebola and HIV/AIDS, grab our attention as they kill many people, especially in the developing world. However, TB has certainly not gone away.

In early December of 2014, doctors tested students at Westside High School in Augusta, Georgia, for tuberculosis after a student was confirmed to have the disease and had been quarantined. More than two hundred students who had contact with the infected person were tested. Health officials said they were confident the infection hadn't spread. This case is not isolated. The Georgia Department of Health sent out a report stating that there were 339 new cases of tuberculosis in the state in 2013.

Not long after the infection was reported in Augusta, another was reported in Duval County, Florida. Raines High School officials advised parents that a student from the school had been sick for months and had been misdiagnosed. The student's illness was confirmed as TB. Health officials rushed to

A refugee in Myanmar suffers from tuberculosis, a disease that afflicts nine million people around the world. The problem is biggest in developing countries.

get everyone who had contact with the ill child tested before students went on their holiday break.

Tuberculosis doesn't frighten people as it once did in places such as the United States because it can be treated. Since the invention of the microscope, humans have been able to see the causes of infectious diseases. Many diseases are caused by **microorganisms** called **bacteria**. Scientists have developed vaccines to kill these bacteria and prevent people from catching several diseases. By the middle of the twentieth century, plagues no longer troubled the rich nations of the world. But still doctors take TB very seriously.

A man was jailed in Georgia in December 2014 for refusing treatment for tuberculosis. The man reportedly went nine months without taking his medication and could have exposed many people to the disease. Someone unknowingly exposed to tuberculosis could be in grave danger. The **World Health Organization** (WHO) reported that in 2013, TB sickened nine million people worldwide. This led to 1.5 million deaths. Among these, 95 percent were from middle- and low-income countries.

Nature is infinitely more resourceful than human ingenuity, and can thwart efforts to battle infectious diseases. In the last fifty years, new plagues have appeared: AIDS has already killed millions throughout the world while Ebola has exacted a terrible toll in lost lives in Africa.

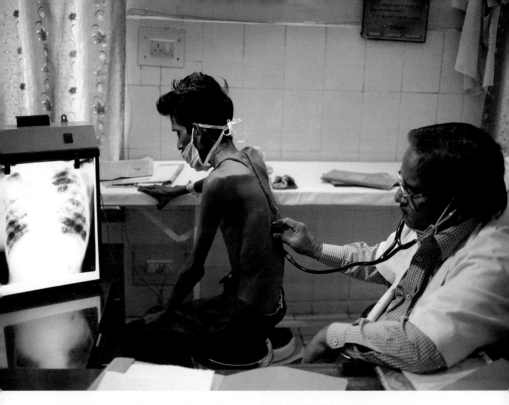

A doctor examines a tuberculosis patient in India, where about 300,000 people die each year from the disease.

The cure of tuberculosis was one of the greatest medical stories of the twentieth century. However, the illness returned at that century's close, renewing its threat to people everywhere. In a wicked twist, it teamed with AIDS to be even more deadly than before. One-fourth of all deaths among people who have tested positive for HIV are caused by TB.

The WHO stated that TB "is second only to HIV/AIDS as the greatest killer worldwide due to a single infectious agent." Tuberculosis is a deadly disease that cannot be ignored.

one Ancient Killer

The story sounds as if it came from a script from the television show *Bones*. Scientists examine mummies from ancient Egypt and discover a probable cause of death: tuberculosis.

Similar discoveries have been made in India and China. *Mycobacterium tuberculosis*, the bacteria that causes the illness, is estimated to be between fifteen thousand and twenty thousand years old. The skeleton of an Egyptian girl from about 3000 BCE shows clear signs of the effects of TB on her bones, resulting in the characteristic hunched back. She suffered what is known today as Pott's disease, or spinal tuberculosis.

In India, hymns were consecrated to the cure of the disease as early as 2000 BCE. Tuberculosis was already infecting people in the Americas by 2000 BCE, 3,500 years before Christopher Columbus crossed the Atlantic. Scientists recently discovered evidence that

Evidence of tuberculosis was found in mummies discovered in ancient burial sites in Peru.

the bacteria were carried from their source in Africa to South America by seals.

Tuberculosis is caused by a bacterium that lives in the soil. It spreads to humans most commonly when they either breathe dusty air in which the bacteria lives or air that is coughed out by an infected person, or drink the milk of an infected cow.

In ancient times, long before humans began to live in cities, the disease may have infected some people. However, the groups of these early humans were so small and far apart, the disease could not reach **epidemic** proportions. The disease would tend to die out as soon as it had killed most of one group of people. But when humans began to settle and grow crops, and build towns, villages, and cities, contact between large groups became common enough for the disease to spread from population to population before it died out.

Throughout the world, the most common name for the disease has been consumption. This name refers to the **pulmonary** (lung) form of the disease. It is called consumption because of the way people who have the disease waste away: as if they are being consumed or eaten from the inside. The name remained accurate even when medical science grew advanced enough to see the actual effects of the disease on the body: for TB eats away at the body's organs and bones. The ancient inhabitants of India called it *yakshma* and the ancient Hebrews

Tuberculosis didn't affect widespread populations until people began building cities.

called it *schanhepeth*. The Old Testament book of Deuteronomy warned that if the Israelites did not follow God's commands, he would smite them with "the consumption."

The ancient Greeks were also familiar with tuberculosis, which they called *phthisis* (a name that continued to be used for the disease even in the nineteenth century), a word derived either from the Greek word meaning "to spit" (referring to the coughing up or spitting of blood in patients with pulmonary TB) or from the word meaning "to consume." The great Greek physician Hippocrates, who lived from around 460 to around 377 BCE and is known as "the father of medicine," described tuberculosis so clearly that his description of the disease is essentially the same one used to diagnose it today.

Hippocrates accurately described tuberculosis nearly 2,400 years ago.

Another Greek physician, Galen, who lived in the Roman Empire from about 131 to 199 CE, also described tuberculosis. He believed that the disease was infectious, and thought that the best treatment was fresh milk; breathing dry, open air; living at a high altitude; and sea voyages. It would take eighteen hundred years to discover any better treatment.

During the Middle Ages, tuberculosis became less common. This may be due to the fact a person who gets infected with leprosy, known today as Hansen's disease, becomes immune to TB. Since Hansen's disease was much more common in Europe during the Middle Ages, fewer people caught TB.

Tuberculosis is an infectious disease that comes in numerous forms. Each form of TB attacks a different part of the body, from the bones and the spine to the intestines. A particularly deadly form of the disease, miliary tuberculosis, occurs when TB spreads into the bloodstream and is carried throughout the body. The most familiar form of tuberculosis, however, is pulmonary tuberculosis—tuberculosis of the lungs.

Tuberculosis attacks whatever area of the body it invades, eating away at it and leaving gaping holes in flesh and bone. It can cause the bones of the spine to weaken and collapse, leaving the infected person with a permanently hunched back. In the lungs, it feeds on the delicate tissues that take oxygen from the air and filter it into the blood. The area develops large cavities, some filled with a cheesy matter and many with pus. As more and more of the lungs are destroyed, the infected person becomes weaker. He or she has trouble breathing; coughs constantly; and suffers from high fever, night sweats, and a loss of appetite. Eventually the TB will eat into one of the many small blood vessels that run throughout the lungs. The infected person will then have the disease's most terrifying symptom: coughing up blood. If the disease continues unchecked, it may eat into one of the arteries—major blood vessels that carry blood away from the heart—and rupture it, causing a hemorrhage, or heavy, uncontrolled internal bleeding. This is usually the cause of death in TB sufferers. Even without a fatal hemorrhage, the person will become weaker, losing weight until he or she dies.

Although TB has a long history throughout the world, it was particularly common in Europe and America during the eighteenth and nineteenth centuries. During that time, the disease was the leading cause of death in all age groups. (This remained true even during the early twentieth century.) This is thought to be because of the growth of cities in those regions during this period. In these cities, population became dense, and many people lived in dirty and cramped conditions. Like any airborne disease, TB spreads much faster when people are gathered in crowds.

Doctors wore beaked masks to ward off the plague and TB.

Tuberculosis became known as the White Plague, to contrast it against the other great plague of European history, the Black Death of the fourteenth century.

Some idea of how common and horrifying TB was in the nineteenth century can be found in the literature, art, and music of the time. Many novels and plays of the period have at least one character whom the disease prevents from living "happily ever after." Two of the most famous heroines in opera—Violetta (in Verdi's *La Traviata*) and Mimi (in Puccini's *La Boheme*)—suffer from the disease, leaving behind mourning lovers. One of the most tragic aspects of tuberculosis was that it killed many people in the prime of their life. Even today, the majority of people infected with the disease are young adults.

Tuberculosis killed young and old. It killed slowly, often not even showing any symptoms until the end. It killed swiftly, striking some of its victims down in a period of a few months. There was no cure and almost no way to treat the disease to stop its growth. It was a terror so common that it became a part of ordinary life. As the nineteenth century drew to close, many scientists and doctors were dedicating their lives to finding a cure for the disease. It would take more than fifty years for them to succeed.

A Closer History

3000 BCE Tuberculosis infects people in Egypt

2000 BCE Earliest written references to the disease in India

460 BCE Hippocrates is born

700 Signs of tuberculosis infection discovered in mummies of humans in Peru

1720 Benjamin Martin suggests that tuberculosis is infectious, something it took years to prove

1796 Edward Jenner invents the smallpox vaccine

1865 Jean-Antoine Villemin infects a rabbit with tuberculosis from an infected cadaver's tissue

1882 Robert Koch discovers tuberculosis bacteria

1889 Koch creates tuberculin

1905 Koch wins Nobel Prize

1921 Creation of the Bacillus Calmette–Guérin (BCG) vaccine

1928 Discovery of penicillin

1933 Gerhard Domagk introduces Prontosil

1943 Selman Waksman discovers **streptomycin**

1943 PAS synthesized by Jorgen Lehmann

Dr. Selman Waksman discovered an antibiotic that treats TB.

1947 Domagk introduces Conteben

1960 Professor John Crofton proposes a combination of three drugs to battle tuberculosis, which proves to reduce TB notifications by 50 percent in three years

1985 Tuberculosis increases in the United States for the first time in more than thirty years

1986 Relationship between tuberculosis and AIDS first described

1990 Strain W emerges in New York; multidrug-resistant (MDR) tuberculosis cases become more common

2002 The global rate of TB cases reaches its high of 141 cases per 100,000 persons

2010 Gene Xpert molecular test, a breakthrough in TB diagnosis, is introduced

2014 Antiretroviral treatment shown to reduce mortality when given during TB therapy; antidiabetic drug increases effectiveness of TB drugs without inducing **resistance** to those drugs

two Feared Disease

T hroughout history, you can say that it was good to be the king. That was the case unless a lot of your subjects had scrofula and people thought you could cure them by touching their necks.

That was the situation in the Middle Ages, when scrofula was common. Scrofula is a condition where the neck is infected with TB, causing it to swell without becoming painful. It was believed that kings were chosen by God to lead their countries, so they would have the power to heal sick people by touching them, just as Jesus had done. Scrofula was particularly singled out for this treatment and became known as the "King's Evil." The French king Louis XIV was said to have touched 2,500 people. Charles II of England was said to have touched 92,000 people between 1662 and 1682. The last English monarch to follow this practice was Queen Anne, who ruled England from 1702 to 1714.

Queen Anne of England reaches to give a young Samuel Johnson a curing touch.

Among her "patients" was the famous Dr. Samuel Johnson, who suffered from scrofula as a young boy and was touched by the Queen in 1712. This did not seem to have any effect. Several years later he had an operation to drain the swellings on his neck and was eventually cured of the disease.

Royalty, of course, had no effect on TB, which became more common as the cities of Europe grew. True consumption, rather than scrofula or its other forms, reemerged during this time. King Louis XIII of France died of the disease in 1643. Tuberculosis also claimed the life of the great philosopher Spinoza in 1677. During the 1600s, TB was infecting people in London at nearly twice the rate that AIDS infects people in the United States today. Tuberculosis was more common than almost any other killer infectious disease, and more feared than any other disease, with the possible exception of the Black Death, which had its last outbreak in England in the 1660s. So terrifying was the disease that the English religious writer John Bunyan called tuberculosis "the Captain of the men of Death."

The Captain would move on to become the deadliest disease in Europe, and it would claim some of the continent's most famous people.

Inoculation and Vaccination

Inoculation is the technique of artificially infecting a person with just enough of a disease to make them sick but not enough to kill them. Once the person has

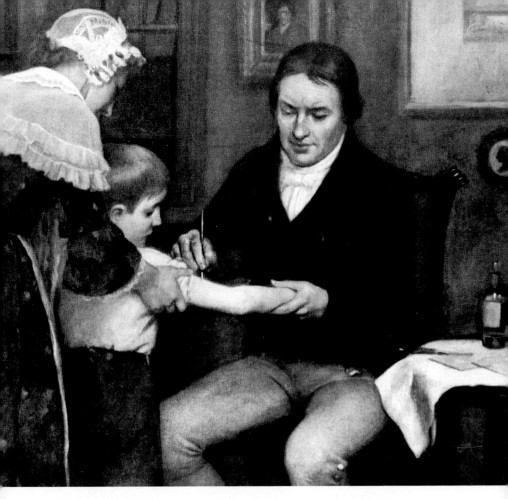

Dr. Edward Jenner was an English surgeon who pioneered the use of vaccination for smallpox.

recovered, he or she will then be immune to the disease. The Chinese had used powdered smallpox scabs, blown up the nose of a patient with a tube, to inoculate people from smallpox for centuries. In the Middle East, the method used was to scratch the patient's arm with a quill that had been dipped in powdered scabs. In the 1700s, the practice was introduced into Great Britain. Soon, inoculation was common for those who could afford it.

A Western Holiday

Tuberculosis is an indirect cause of one of the great legends of the Wild West. John Henry "Doc" Holliday is primarily remembered for his role in the Gunfight at the O.K. Corral in Tombstone, Arizona, in 1881. His goal as a young man was not to be a gunfighter—he wanted to become a dentist.

Holliday attended the Pennsylvania College of Dental Surgery in 1872 and returned to his home state of Georgia to set up a practice in Atlanta. He developed a cough, which was diagnosed as TB. Doctors advised Holliday to move out West to take advantage of the region's drier air. He settled in Dallas, Texas, where he developed a reputation more for his skills at poker than at dentistry. He was arrested for taking part in a gunfight, and began a living as a drifter who earned his money gambling.

Despite his lifestyle, he became friends with Marshall Wyatt Earp. He stood with Wyatt and Virgil Earp during the gunfight in which three men died. Three other men, including Holliday, were wounded in the melee.

Holliday did not fare as well against TB. A life of gambling and drinking caused his health to deteriorate rapidly. By 1887, he went

Statues of Doc Holliday and Wyatt Earp stand in front of the Tucson Rail Depot.

for treatment in the fresh air and the hot mineral baths in Glenwood Springs, Colorado. Those baths were supposed to help people with consumption, but they didn't help Holliday. He died that same year on November 8. He was only thirty-six. However, had he not contracted tuberculosis he may have stayed in Georgia and practiced dentistry, and he would not have become a part of American history.

Those baths remain in Glenwood Springs. They can do wonders for one's body after a hard day of skiing at nearby Aspen Mountain.

Inoculation, however, had some serious drawbacks. After inoculation, the patient would develop a mild case of the disease, and sometimes he or she still died from it. During the period of this illness, the patient was highly contagious. What was needed was a method to gain the resistance inoculation brought without the risks of contagion or death.

An English doctor, Edward Jenner, thought he might have a solution. Among dairy farmers it was said that people who caught cowpox, a smallpox-like disease of cows that did not kill humans, could not catch smallpox. In 1796, Jenner was able to inoculate a boy with cowpox taken from a milkmaid. The boy did not become seriously ill, and later was found to be immune to smallpox. Jenner had found the magic shield against smallpox infection. He called his technique **vaccination**, from the Latin words meaning "taken from a cow." Jenner's discovery led to the eventual eradication of smallpox in 1977.

Later researchers, such as Louis Pasteur, discovered how to make a weakened form of a deadly **virus**. Pasteur used this form of microorganisms to inoculate people, who would then be immune to the disease. Such techniques were used to create a tuberculosis vaccine known as BCG. This vaccine has been used in many parts of the world with some success. However, it has not been widely used in the United States.

Patron of Artists

English poet John Keats was born in 1795. In his boyhood he was an excellent student and an active athlete who enjoyed sports, including boxing. When he was fourteen, his mother died of TB. Keats nursed her during her final days, and may have caught the disease from her.

After his mother's death, Keats decided to study medicine. In 1816, at the age of twenty-one, he became licensed to practice medicine. (He was not a doctor. At the time, a doctorate in medicine was not required to treat people.) However, he was already becoming more interested in poetry than medicine, and he never actually became a physician.

In 1818, Keats began to display the first symptoms of TB. His health suffered, but he continued to work. In 1819, he produced some of his greatest poems, including the famous "Ode on a Grecian Urn."

In 1820, he began to cough up blood. With his medical training, he knew that this was a death sentence, even though his personal physician was convinced that he did not have tuberculosis. The disease progressed rapidly. Keats soon became extremely weak. He took a number of sea voyages and, at the urging of his friend Percy Bysshe Shelley, decided to go to Italy. There the climate was believed to help TB patients. He was severely ill throughout the voyage, coughing up blood frequently.

Keats lived for only three months once he arrived in Italy, dying in Rome on February 21, 1821. This was just over a year from the time his first major symptom appeared for TB. Some consider Keats to have been the greatest English poet since Shakespeare. His story is tragic not only because of the speed of his illness, but also because his fate was common for generations of young people throughout the nineteenth century.

Fatal to the Family

The story of the Brontë family is noteworthy for depicting how tuberculosis could ravage an entire family. It also lends insight into why many people believed the disease to be hereditary.

Patrick Brontë, the father, was a Methodist minister who is believed to have suffered from TB for most of his life. His wife, Maria, died in 1820, after giving birth to their youngest daughter, Anne, who later became a famous writer. Although there are questions regarding the cause of her death, many facts point to TB.

In 1825, one of the Brontë children, also named Maria, died from TB at the age of twelve. Within a month, her sister, Elizabeth, died from it as well. She was eleven years old.

The family suffered no more from TB until 1848, when both Emily Brontë (also a famous writer) and Branwell, the only son, died of the disease within three months of each other. Two weeks after Emily's death, Anne was diagnosed as also having TB. She died

Writers Anne, Emily, and Charlotte Brontë all died of TB, as did brother Branwell, who painted this portrait in 1834.

in 1849. Charlotte Brontë (a famous writer as well) survived until 1855, when she died of a wasting disease that most probably was TB. Their father lived to be eighty-five years old.

Extreme experiences such as that of the Brontë family were not uncommon at the time. Children of parents with tuberculosis often died of the disease. Today we know that this is because the close contact among family members promotes the spread of the TB bacteria. But until the bacterium was discovered, no one could even prove that TB was infectious. Thus, cases such as that of the Brontës helped reinforce the idea that the disease was inherited.

Tuberculosis became associated with artistic genius, because so many great writers, poets, and musicians died of it. In addition to Charlotte Brontë, author of *Jane Eyre*, and Keats, the list of artists included Robert Louis Stevenson, author of *Treasure Island*; Anton Chekhov, the great Russian playwright and short-story writer; Frederic Chopin, the great pianist and composer; and George Orwell, the author of *1984*. It was thought that somehow artists were more susceptible to the disease because of heredity or that being an artist somehow made one more likely to contract the disease. However, it seems more likely that the unhealthy and impoverished conditions that many artists lived in was the real reason the disease was so common among them. Still, images of the solitary artist or writer (gaunt and thin, eyes burning with feverish inspiration—all symptoms of tuberculosis) became a popular myth, and survive in some form to the present day.

Latent Illness

One of the characteristics of TB is that only 10 percent of the people who become infected by the bacteria get sick. And of those who do, the bacteria can remain in their system for many years before symptoms appear.

This is what happened to former first lady Eleanor Roosevelt, who died on November 7, 1962, in New York City at age seventy-eight. She had been an outstanding activist on behalf of the rights of the poor, minorities, and women. Eleanor Roosevelt remains revered as the greatest first lady in US history because she worked hard to further the policies of her husband, President Franklin Delano Roosevelt. The first lady also fought publicly for policies her husband was against— if she felt strongly for them. Because the president suffered from polio—a disease that attacks the nervous system—which had left him paralyzed from the waist down, Eleanor Roosevelt frequently toured the nation, reporting back to him on the various conditions in which people lived.

After the president's death in 1945, Eleanor was made a delegate to the United Nations, where she helped to write the Universal Declaration on Human Rights. She remained an internationally famous figure, meeting with many of the most important world leaders of the time until the day she died. By all accounts, her life was active and rewarding, yet she was

Eleanor Roosevelt, shown speaking in 1950, carried tuberculosis
in her body while leading an active and productive life.

struck down by a disease that over time diminishes a healthy body.

Eleanor Roosevelt had contracted TB as a young woman while visiting France. She apparently recovered from this early infection, and went on to lead an extremely active life. But the disease remained hidden in her body and reemerged during her latter years. Eleanor Roosevelt died of a disease she had caught almost fifty years before her death.

Eleanor Roosevelt's life illustrates many of the unusual and frustrating elements of TB, a disease that many believe has killed more people throughout history than any other. She was born during the time TB was still a common infection and the leading cause of death. She lived through the period of exciting discoveries about this mysterious illness, including the discovery of the "miracle drugs" that finally made TB curable.

Eleanor Roosevelt wasn't diagnosed with TB until the final weeks of her life. She had what is known as military tuberculosis, which affected her major organs. This form of the disease is rare, striking only about 1 percent of those who contract it. Another unusual factor in her case was that the drugs that cured others had no effect on her illness. Drugs used today are able to treat the disease even if the patient has developed immunity to some **antibiotics**.

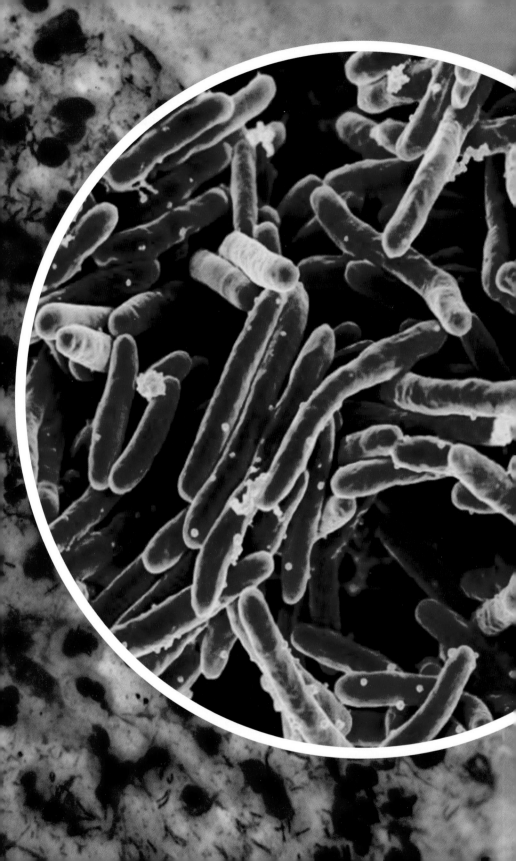

three Finding the Cause

R eal advancement in the treatment of tuberculosis didn't come until the end of the nineteenth century.

Robert Koch made the first big treatment discovery in 1882. He discovered the tubercle bacilli that caused tuberculosis. And in 1885, Wilhelm Roentgen developed the X-ray, which help diagnose the disease. For the first time ever, the inner workings of the body could be made visible without having to cut into the flesh. This discovery allowed doctors to diagnose patients earlier and isolated them sooner so the disease could not spread.

To understand why it took so long to discover a cure for TB, it is crucial to learn more about the disease's many peculiar characteristics. Some of these kept their true nature hidden from science for centuries.

This is an electron micrograph scan of the Mycobacterium tuberculosis bacteria that cause the disease.

Tuberculosis is caused by bacteria called *Mycobacterium tuberculosis.* Bacteria are microscopic organisms. Many bacteria live on dead animals and plants, and help cause the process known as rotting or decomposition. Others live inside living animals and plants. Many are relatively harmless, and a few are even helpful, such as the bacteria that live inside a human intestine and help digest some foods. But some bacteria have the ability to cause disease in animals and plants—and *Mycobacterium tuberculosis* is one of the worst of these.

The TB bacterium is one of the hardiest kinds of bacteria in the world. It can survive in the soil for months without nourishment. Its rod-like shape is enclosed in a tough capsule of material that is difficult to destroy. This is one of the reasons that TB is so difficult to cure. Normally, the body's natural defenses can destroy invading germs by using specialized cells that surround and consume them. But the tough outer shell or "capsule" of the tuberculosis bacteria cannot be destroyed by these defenses, allowing it to grow with little resistance.

Tuberculosis reproduces asexually but it doesn't grow rapidly. It divides once every fifteen to twenty hours. By comparison, *Escherichia coli* divides every twenty minutes, making *E. coli* a rapidly moving pathogen. One of the challenges to finding the bacteria was finding a way to make it grow outside of the body so it could be studied. The slow way in which TB spreads is the reason that people who come down with the disease will sometimes not show any symptoms for many years. It is also why others who show symptoms can live for a long time with the disease.

The body's defenses form a hard wall around the invading bacteria. These tiny spots are called tubercles, which gives the disease its name. In most people, walling the bacteria up will keep it from spreading. However, in others this isn't enough. This happens especially if they have repeated contact with the disease. The infection continues to grow, killing cells in its path. The tubercles expand and merge, eventually causing holes called lesions in the affected organs. In the lungs this often results in the rupture of a blood vessel, which can cause death.

Because it can take so long for the disease to develop, many people thought that tuberculosis was not infectious. Some people felt that the disease was hereditary, or passed down genetically from a person's parents. This was because some families had many more people with the disease than others. Today we know that family members living with an infected person are at a much greater risk of catching the disease. Also, some people have inherited a greater susceptibility to TB. Regardless, one must have contact with the bacteria in order to contract the disease.

Seeing the Invisible

Wilhelm Roentgen was a scientist of some renown, but he made his most important discovery by accident in November of 1895. He noticed that some invisible ray generated by a Crookes tube (a cathode-ray tube that emits electrons) passed through cardboard he had wrapped around the tube and made a nearby fluorescent screen glow. He then put other objects between the tube and the screen and observed that they blocked the ray in variable degrees according to their density. On an impulse, he passed his hand in front of the ray, which he called an X-ray, and saw that it passed through his skin and showed the bones beneath it on the screen.

A few days later he took a photograph of an X-ray of his wife's hand as proof, thus starting the practice of radiology.

Tuberculosis is revealed in two ways in an X-ray. When the TB bacteria enter the lungs, white blood cells called microphages surround them to wall them off. This prevents them from activating, but it causes scarring in the lungs and shows up as white spots on an X-ray. If the bacteria get loose and reactivate in the lungs, a cavity can form. This is an ideal place for the bacteria to reproduce, and this helps destroy the lung tissue. These cavities also show up in an X-ray.

An X-ray doesn't positively identify

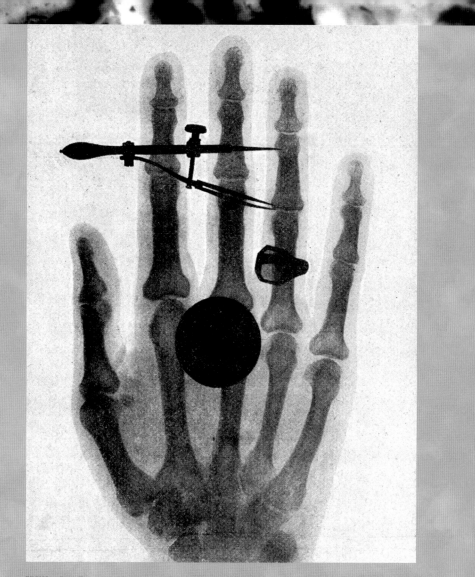

Wilhelm Roentgen took this photo of an X-ray of his wife's hand.

the presence of TB in a person. It can be confirmed only if the bacteria are found in a sample taken from that person. However, the X-ray made early detection of TB possible, and it was used for this purpose by 1900.

Drinking milk from an infected cow was a common way to get TB.

Another reason it took so long to identify the cause of TB was that there were several ways that the disease could be contracted. It is possible to catch it from some animals. The most common way of doing so is to drink the milk of a cow infected with bovine, or cow-related, TB. (The disease was fairly common among cattle until the development of an effective vaccine and widespread pasteurization of milk made it exceptionally rare in Europe and America.) Tuberculosis can also be caught from breathing air that contains the bacteria—usually from a sick person or from dusty, bacteria-filled air.

The final reason it took so long to discover the cause of TB is that for most of human history, people thought that it was impossible that something too small for the eye to see could harm a person. Only after the development of the microscope in the late seventeenth century was it even possible to see these tiny bacteria. Still it took more than a century to finally prove that some of them caused diseases.

As late as the 1880s, many reputable scientists thought that TB was an inherited disease. Robert Koch believed otherwise, and spent much of his life in pursuit to discover the cause of, and the cure for, the disease.

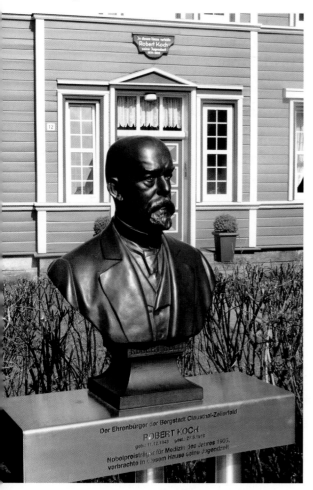

Koch was born in Germany in 1843. He became a medical doctor at the age of twenty-three. In 1876, he proved that specific bacteria caused the sheep disease anthrax. This was an amazing achievement, given the technology of the day. Next, he focused on TB. In 1882, Koch was the first to identify

A statue of Dr. Robert Koch stands in front of his childhood home in Germany.

the bacteria that caused the disease. This discovery caused a sensation. For the first time, the cause of TB had been discovered. His name became a household word almost immediately. Famous, and by this time supported by the German government, Koch continued to search for a cure for the disease. In 1889, he announced that he had found a substance that killed the bacteria and did not harm the body. This was tuberculin, made from an extract of dead tuberculosis bacteria. Unfortunately, further experiments showed that the substance did not stop the growth of the bacteria. Other scientists discovered that if a person had an allergic reaction to tuberculin that was scratched into their skin, it meant they had been infected with TB. This formed the basis of the TB test that we use today.

Koch's Postulates

In the course of his research into the cause of tuberculosis, Koch perfected the method known as "pure culture." This is where a certain type of bacteria was grown without contamination from any other bacteria. This made it possible to test which bacteria caused which disease.

At about this time, Koch formulated his four postulates, or claims, for determining which microorganism causes a particular disease.

- The microorganism must be found in every case of the disease, existing in a relationship with the damaged tissue of the patient in a way that explains that damage.
- The microorganism must be grown in a pure culture outside the patient.
- This culture must be able to produce in healthy animals an illness identical in all respects to the original disease.
- The microorganism must then be recovered from the infected animals.

Koch rigorously applied these postulates to his own research, and they have since become the standards for determining the cause of any infectious disease. However, they also show how difficult it is to determine the precise cause of a disease.

Koch never succeeded in finding a cure for tuberculosis, although his work on the disease resulted in his winning the Nobel Prize in 1905. Although many scientists carried on his work after his death in 1910, the cure for tuberculosis was still more than thirty-five years away.

four New Approach

Robert Koch's discovery of the cause of TB came years before an effective treatment was developed. Ideas in how to fight the disease ranged from the inventive to the bizarre to the extreme.

One idea that had some merit was started in 1859 by Hermann Brehmer in Silesia, which is now mostly in Poland. He said that patients should be isolated in a sanatorium, and his idea caught on. Sanatoriums were set up in the rural or mountainous areas. There, people with TB seemed to do better in the thin and dry air, or by the seashore. In some places, the belief that cold, dry air would be beneficial was taken to an almost ridiculous extreme. Students were made to study outside in the middle of winter, wearing shorts and no shirt.

Surgical treatments, such as removing the diseased part of the lung, were dangerous and of limited value. None were very effective in helping people with advanced cases of TB.

The Trudeau Sanitarium in Saranac Lake, New York, was used to treat TB patients until a cure was found.

What was needed was a method of killing the bacteria without harming the patient. Yet for many years, little research was done in this area. This was because many scientists felt that the best method of combating any disease was to create a vaccine for it so that people could not catch it. Two French scientists, Albert Calmette and Camille Guérin, had created a weakened form of the TB bacteria called BCG that could be used to create a vaccine. However, there had been problems with the vaccine. Because of poor quality control, samples of it used to combat a TB epidemic in Germany actually spread the disease. Also, some scientists and public health officials, especially in the United States, did not think the vaccine was effective enough. Because of this, and the difficulties in producing vaccines for other common bacterial infections, attention began to turn toward creating drug therapies. The problem was to find a way to kill only the disease-causing bacteria and not the other cells of the body.

In 1933, Gerhard Domagk, a German doctor working for Bayer laboratories, and his chemist colleague, Josef Klarer, created a new drug called Prontosil. Although it did not affect tuberculosis, Prontosil cured many infections, such as blood poisoning, that had previously been impossible to treat. Soon, other researchers had broken down the chemical structure of Prontosil. Based on their findings, they produced even more effective drugs called sulfa drugs. Sulfa drugs are synthetic antibiotics, and were the first chemical substances used to treat bacterial infections.

Selman Waksman, Gerhard Domagk (standing), and Sir Alexander Fleming all received the Nobel Prize.

Five years before the creation of Prontosil, in 1928, British doctor Alexander Fleming discovered that bacterial cultures died when they came in contact with a common bread mold. This mold, *Penicillium notatum*, produced a substance that came to be known as penicillin. Unfortunately, problems in mass-producing penicillin prevented it from making a real impact in the world of medicine until the 1940s.

However, the discovery that one naturally occurring antibiotic existed prompted many researchers to look for others. At Rutgers University in New Jersey, a **microbiologist** named Dr. Selman Waksman began performing experiments to find an organism that could kill the tuberculosis bacteria. A specialist in the area of soil microbiology, Wasksman was particularly suited for this task because TB lives in the soil. However, since it is not found everywhere, he theorized that there must be some other organism capable of killing it.

Future Development

George Orwell is best known for writing about a futuristic society. The tragedy is that if he had been born a little later than 1903, he might not have died of tuberculosis. George Orwell was the pen name of the English writer Eric Blair, author of the novels *1984* and *Animal Farm*.

Orwell began to display symptoms of tuberculosis in 1938, although initial tests for the disease were negative. In 1947, he finally was diagnosed with tuberculosis and was admitted to a hospital. There he was treated with streptomycin but developed strange reactions to it. His skin turned red and itchy. Blisters blossomed across his lips, cheeks, and throat. His hair and nails fell out. After fifty days, the doctors were forced to take him off of the drug. However, his tuberculosis was much improved, and he returned to work on *1984*. Soon, though, the strain of completing the book resulted in a relapse. Streptomycin no longer had any effect on his disease, and he died on January 22, 1950.

Orwell had an allergy to streptomycin, which kept the doctors from completing his treatment the first time. Because of this, his infection had become resistant to the drug, which could no longer help him. He may have been saved if he had been treated with multiple drugs, but that was not the path taken by doctors at the time of his death.

Multiple drug treatments for TB came too late to save George Orwell.

In 1943, one of Waksman's research assistants, Albert Schatz, found that a strange organism, not quite a fungus or a bacteria, produced a substance that definitely killed the tuberculosis bacteria. The discovery of this substance, streptomycin, was a breakthrough in antibiotic technology.

Early tests on streptomycin were spectacular. Patients with advanced forms of the disease almost immediately improved. They rapidly regained weight, their cough disappeared, and their lungs began to heal. Completely bedridden patients were suddenly walking around. Streptomycin had proven to be a medical miracle.

Two other tuberculosis-fighting drugs were introduced at the same time as streptomycin. Conteben, created by Gerhard Domagk, was made by manipulating Prontosil molecules until the new configuration could kill TB. PAS, or para-amino salt, is a modification of the common aspirin molecule, discovered by the Swedish doctor Jorgen Lehmann. Both Conteben and PAS proved to be effective against TB, although neither was as powerful as streptomycin. It was fortunate that all three were discovered so close together. It soon became apparent that one anti-tuberculosis drug was not enough to defeat this stubborn disease.

The case for using multiple drugs at the same time to treat the disease was not made clear until 1960. Professor John Crofton at the University of Edinburgh said streptomycin, PAS, and Isoniazid should be taken together to combat the disease from the start. People doubted this approach until it was proven effective in a large international trial.

The reason this approach works is that bacteria can become resistant to antibiotics. Scientists were finding that in people who suffered a relapse of TB, bacteria in their body were no longer affected by streptomycin. When a person has been infected with TB, they will have millions of bacteria in their body. A vast majority of these will be killed by one drug, but a very small amount of these bacteria change and become immune to one or another of the drugs. If only one drug is introduced into the patient, the **resistant bacteria** will survive and continue to multiply. Eventually, the patient will relapse.

Crofton's approach solved this problem. Using multiple drugs killed all of the bacteria.

Soon, new drugs were produced that were even more powerful than streptomycin. Tuberculosis death rates began to plummet. What had been the leading cause of death in humans for centuries vanished in the course of mere decades.

It appeared as if the battle against TB had been won. Then, bacteria began to fight back and renewed the struggle.

five Multiple Threats

F acing an enemy that is changing has challenged scientists in their efforts to eliminate tuberculosis. The emergence of multiple drug-resistant (MDR) strains of tuberculosis is a serious threat to the public health of every country in the world. One strain, called Strain W, is resistant to four of the major tuberculosis drugs. It first appeared in three New York City hospitals in 1990 and rapidly spread across the United States. New York suffered a 38 percent increase in TB cases from 1989 to 1990, and many of the cases were caused by this particularly dangerous strain of TB.

Infections in the United States reached a high in 1992. A task force was assembled and it put together a plan to fight the outbreaks of multidrug-resistant (MDR) tuberculosis. Its programs had two goals: to find people with active TB cases and to treat them with effective drugs, thereby keeping those infected from spreading the disease; and to preventively treat

Kenyans march to encourage donations to fight AIDS, tuberculosis, and malaria in 2009.

people who have a latent case of TB (worldwide this is one-third of the population) and are at high risk of developing the disease. The task force also sought to find ways to control infection, and set up training programs for healthcare workers.

The plan has worked. The Centers for Disease Control and Prevention (CDC) reported that the number of deaths from TB each year in the United States had fallen to 536, or 69 percent, between 1992 and 2011.

There have been other advances. It was discovered that the tuberculosis bacteria had evolved so it could work against the body's natural defenses. The body uses alveolar macrophages, which are white blood cells in our lungs, to engulf the TB bacteria. These macrophages then die, keeping their membrane intact and trapping the bacteria inside. This is called **apoptosis**. However, the tuberculosis bacteria have found a way to influence the macrophages so they undergo a cell death called necrosis. In this form, the membrane breaks, allowing the bacteria to escape. Scientists have been working with molecules called eicosanoids that can prevent necrosis.

Scientists have also discovered that Metformin, an old anti-diabetic drug, keeps the bacteria from reproducing. This can keep the infection from spreading and prevents the bacteria from becoming resistant to drugs.

These developments have helped treat and prevent tuberculosis in the United States, but the disease is still a major threat in other parts of the world. It was estimated that 480,000 people developed multidrug-resistant TB in 2013. When people immigrate into new areas such as the United States, they sometimes carry the disease with them, and then spread it. According to the CDC, 65 percent of the TB cases reported in the United States in 2013 occurred in people who were born in a foreign country.

The worst factor involved in the return of TB, however, is HIV/AIDS, a disease that destroys the body's natural **immune system**. A person who has HIV/AIDS dies not from the virus, but from the infections that attack his or her weakened defenses. Only 10 percent of all people infected with the TB bacteria will develop the disease. However, people with HIV/AIDS are twenty-six to thirty-one times more likely to develop TB. One quarter of all HIV/AIDS-related deaths are caused by TB.

Like tuberculosis, HIV/AIDS usually takes several years to kill a person who is infected with it. Often, symptoms will not be apparent for many years. However, a person infected with both HIV/AIDS and TB can die very rapidly. The two diseases seem to mutually support each other, each one making the other work faster and more viciously. Even worse, people who have TB and HIV/AIDS often develop strains of TB that are resistant to drugs. This is because their natural defenses have been compromised, or weakened, by HIV/AIDS. Even with the help of

Those at Risk

Tuberculosis is a curable disease. There are several things people do that can increase their risk of contracting the disease or dying from it. One is that people with the disease fail to take all of their medication after they begin

A long-lasting cough is one symptom of tuberculosis.

to feel better. As a result, strains of bacteria that are resistant to one or more of the drugs eventually reinfect them. Worse, they can spread these resistant strains to other people.

Also, smoking contributes to 20 percent of all TB cases worldwide. It makes people more susceptible to the disease, less able to fight the infection, and causes treatment to become less effective. Another risk factor is injecting illegal drugs. The most common way of getting TB is to breathe in germs. They can be spread when someone with the infections coughs, laughs, sneezes, sings, or talks. People who have conditions that compromise their immune systems should be diligent about monitoring their health to make sure they haven't become infected with TB. Here are symptoms of tuberculosis:

- a bad cough that lasts three weeks or longer
- chest pain
- coughing up blood or sputum
- feeling weak or fatigued
- weight loss
- loss of appetite
- chills
- fever
- night sweats

antibiotics, their bodies cannot kill all the TB bacteria, allowing the resistant strains to grow even faster than they would normally.

The discovery of effective treatments for TB in the middle of the twentieth century was one of the greatest triumphs in the history of medical science. Mankind's deadliest foe had apparently been conquered, and would no longer trouble the world—or so it seems. Looking back now, we can see that this overconfident attitude has caused a neglect of TB, with dire consequences. As HIV/AIDS ravages many parts of the world, its partner, tuberculosis, is likely to reemerge as one of the leading causes of death in the world.

Still, there is reason for optimism. The death rate due to tuberculosis fell 45 percent between 1990 and 2013, and an estimated thirty-seven million lives were saved by diagnosis and treatment from 2000 and 2013. Eighty percent of the TB cases worldwide came from twenty-two countries. Some of them are recording gains in fighting the illness. For example, in the decade ending in 2013, Cambodia experienced a 50 percent decrease in the prevalence of TB.

There are new two-hour tests that are good at detecting tuberculosis being introduced in many countries. Early detection is key to combatting this killer. With worldwide declines in TB illness, scientists are on track to halt the spread of the disease in 2015.

An AIDS patient with tuberculosis gets comforted in Cambodia, where deaths due to TB have decreased.

However, with TB among the five leading causes of death of women aged fifteen to forty-four and with eighty thousand children dying from the illness each year, there is still a lot of work to be done.

Glossary

antibiotic A drug that kills bacteria. Antibiotics have no effect on viruses.

apoptosis A genetically directed form of cell destruction in which the membrane of the cell remains intact. It is different from necrosis, in which the membrane of the cell breaks.

bacteria Microscopic parasites that infect living hosts and grow inside of them.

epidemic An outbreak of a disease that infects many or most people in a certain area, such a city or country.

immune system The body's natural defenses against diseases.

inoculation Introducing a disease artificially into a person so that they become resistant to that disease.

microbiologist A person who studies microscopic forms of life.

microorganisms A microscopic organism, especially a bacterium, virus, or fungus.

pulmonary Of or relating to the lungs.

resistance The ability of a person to keep from catching a disease. In many cases, once a person has caught the disease, they cannot catch it again.

resistant bacteria Bacteria that have become immune to one or more antibiotics.

streptomycin An antibiotic that treats tuberculosis and other serious infections.

vaccination Inoculating a person with a weakened form of a disease so that a person will become resistant to the disease without either getting sick or infecting others.

virus Microscopic parasites, much smaller than bacteria. They are not "alive" but can only reproduce within a living cell.

World Health Organization The public health arm of the United Nations, which monitors outbreaks of diseases and the performance of global health systems.

For More Information

American Lung Association

www.lung.org/lung-disease/tuberculosis

Learn about this disease, how you can prevent and live with it, and what you can do to help fight it.

National Geographic Health and Human Body

science.nationalgeographic.com/science/health-and-human-body

This website provides information on how the human body works, how diseases affect the body, and links to the latest science news.

World Health Organization Media Centre

www.who.int/mediacentre/factsheets/fs104/en

Get the facts on tuberculosis and its status worldwide, plus find links to stories, publications, and other information.

Interested in learning more about Tuberculosis?
Check out these websites and organizations.

Organizations

American Medical Association (AMA)
515 North State Street
Chicago, IL 60610
(312) 464-5000
www.ama-assn.org

The Centers for Disease Control (CDC)
1600 Clifton Road
Atlanta, GA 30333
(800) 311-3435 or (404) 639-3311
www.cdc.gov

National Foundation of Infectious Disease
4733 Bethesda Avenue, Suite 750
Bethesda, MD 20814
(301) 656-0003
www.nfid.org

National Institute of Allergy and Infectious Diseases
NIAID Office of Communications & Public Liaison
31 Center Drive MSC 2520
Bethesda, MD 20892-2520
(301) 496-1884
www.niaid.nih.gov

For Further Reading

Books

Allman, Tony. *Tuberculosis*. Diseases and Disorders. San Diego, CA: Lucent Books, 2006.

Bynum, Helen. *Spitting Blood: The History of Tuberculosis*. Oxford, UK: Oxford University Press, 2012.

Daniel, Thomas M. *Captain of Death: The Story of Tuberculosis*. Rochester, NY: University of Rochester Press, 1997.

Farrell, Jeanette. *Invisible Enemies: Stories of Infectious Disease*. New York: Farrar, Straus & Giroux, Inc., 1997.

Websites

The Economic Times
"Anti-diabetic drug many help treat tuberculosis: Study"

articles.economictimes.indiatimes.com/2014-12-18 /news/57196227_1_drug-resistance-mycobacterium -tuberculosis-mtb

National Geographic
"Seals May Have Carried Tuberculosis to the New World"

phenomena.nationalgeographic.com/2014/08/20/seals -may-have-carried-tuberculosis-to-the-new-world

Index

Page numbers in **boldface** are illustrations. Entries in **boldface** are glossary terms.

Index

Tuberculosis